GENERATION Z *in the* WORKPLACE

HELPING THE NEWEST GENERATION IN THE WORKFORCE BUILD SUCCESSFUL WORKING RELATIONSHIPS AND CAREER PATHS

DR. CANDACE STEELE FLIPPIN

Generation Z in the Workplace: Helping the Newest Generation in the Workforce Build Successful Working Relationships and Career Paths

By Dr. Candace Steele Flippin

Copyright © 2017 by Candace Steele Flippin. All rights reserved.

Printed in the United States of America
First Printing, 2017

ISBN 978-0-9986384-0-9 Kindle
ISBN 978-0-9986384-1-6 Paperback

Generation Z in the Workplace

Helping the Newest Generation in the Workforce
Build Successful Working Relationships and Career Paths

By Dr. Candace Steele Flippin

What will it take to help Generation Z succeed at work and in their careers?

Further, how can today's managers and employees adjust to a workplace that is getting younger?

Generation Z in the Workplace provides research-based information to help Gen Z workers can get the most out of their roles and careers. Generation Z in the Workplace also offers suggestions for those who supervise members of Gen Z, to help them develop their careers and reach their potential.

Generation Z in the Workplace explores insights from our young, up-and-coming workforce and helps us understand what Gen Z wants from their careers. And, provides information and tools to help them succeed at work.

Dedication

To everyone who wants more out of their career.

Acknowledgments

I'd like to thank my family – Thomas, Stacy, T.J., Vicki, Tony and Renee – for their encouragement to pursue this research topic.

This book is the culmination of the work and efforts of a fantastic team. I'm grateful for everyone who helped with the background research, editing, and support. A very special thanks to Lana, Robert, Nicholas, Zachery, Sammy, Janine, and Marianna for helping me bring my research to life and getting this book over the finish line.

Table of Contents

About this book   xi

Introduction   1

The complex workplace of the 21st Century becomes even more challenging with so many different generation groups.

Chapter One – What Do We Know about Generation Z?   5

Who exactly is Gen Z? What international and domestic events have influenced Gen Z and what generalizations might be made about this cohort? How do these influences play out in the workplace?

Chapter Two – Values   11

What does Gen Z hold to be important, both professionally and personally? How does the American Dream fit into their value system?

Chapter Three – Goals   25

What kind of career goals motivate Gen Z? Do they feel like they are where they want and need to be in order to achieve these goals?

Chapter Four – Work Environment Preferences   37

How are current job opportunities stacking up for Gen Z, according to their own perceptions? What are they thinking about their future employment options? How hard do they want to work and for how long? Is Gen Z invested for the short or long term and why? How do they feel about their boss as a leader?

Chapter Five – Attitudes about Other Generations at Work 59

How does Gen Z really view the older cohorts: Y, X, and the Baby Boomers? How do they in turn view Gen Z?

Chapter Six – Career Advice/Reflection 71

What lessons have Gen Z learned along the way? What advice do they value?

Chapter Seven – Everyone Has Something to Offer 85

So what does this all mean practically, to Gen Z workers and to those who supervise them? How can we leverage this knowledge to succeed?

Action Plan for Gen Z: Summary of Exercises 91

Checklist for Supervisors of Gen Z 99

References 103

About the Author 107

About This Book

At present, there are five people in the labor force between ages 15 and 64 for every person over age 65. By 2050, this ratio will drop to 3:1. This means that we will have fewer workers in the labor force with historical knowledge driving action in the workplace.[1] It can only be to the advantage of supervisors and their employees to explore everything that can be done to prepare up and coming generations for this significant shift. This necessarily includes shaping company and employee success by focusing on the positive and the possible, while avoiding unflattering and inaccurate generalizations.

Generation X, Y, and Z leaders are emerging within the multi-generational workforce as the Baby Boomer generation begins to retire. At the same time, there has been a great deal of discussion about generation gaps and how they are creating challenges in the workplace.

The goal of *Generation Z in the Workplace* is to explore insights from our young, up-and coming workforce and understand what Gen Z want from their careers.

Generation Z in the Workplace provides research-based information about how Gen Z workers can get the most out of their roles and careers. The book also offers suggestions for those who supervise members of Generation Z to help them develop their careers and reach their potential.

This book provides recommendations that are based on my research findings. Some of my research results surprised me. Many of the findings challenged the common, and often negative, perceptions of each generation. And, while my suggestions are not a substitute for hard work and personal commitment or a guarantee for success, my hope is that this information may be a helpful resource for navigating careers and the workplace.

I hope you will read *Generation Z in the Workplace* with an open mind and come away optimistic and hopeful for the future of the workplace and the opportunities ahead.

Everyone has something to offer.

Introduction

The complex workplace of the 21st Century becomes even more challenging with so many different generation groups.

Whenever a new generation enters the workforce, the influx of new people inevitably brings about the potential for both positive and negative change.

Currently, there can be up to five different generation groups employed together in a workplace.

- Traditionalist born 1922-1945
- Baby Boomer born 1946–1964
- Generation X born 1965–1980
- Generation Y (Millennials) born 1981–1995
- Generation Z born after 1995

And the opinions about each group vary greatly from favorable to neutral to negative. The varying media reports along with our own personal experiences with each generation in the workplace are also making many of us question what we are hearing and reading about the different generations.

Out with the old?

While change takes time, it is also important to appreciate that traditional and well-established processes also matter. Sudden shifts in the way work gets done—without being mindful of unintended consequences—can be problematic.

In with the new?

The fast pace of technological and business trends requires us to adapt. Yet, challenges can arise if the work environment does not allow for previous assumptions to be questioned or for new ideas to be adopted.

To that point, in the past year, while interviewing a young professional and a more seasoned executive as part of my research, I was struck by some of their comments.

Gen Y Female

There are so many negative stereotypes about Millennials and there are so many negative articles on Millennials. It's always in my news feed, you know? Millennials think of this or Millennials need to be better at this. I'll read it but then I normally reassure myself that I'm not doing what they say that the Millennials are bad at doing.

Gen X Male

I had to remind myself many times in the last couple of decades that I can't be frustrated with my 25-year-old employees for not being 50 years old. I have to allow them to be 25 and allow and acknowledge that there's learning ahead and don't be too harsh on them as they have lessons and foibles and stumbles. Some of these things that they're doing, that we've done now many times over, they're doing for the first time.

Sound familiar? It made me wonder what can be done to help the various generations—Baby Boomers, Gen X, Gen Y (a.k.a. Millennials), and Gen Z—relate to one another better at work? If people tend to act on preconceived perceptions rather than getting to know each person individually, how does that contribute to conflict and stress in the workplace? And, how can greater awareness of these potential pitfalls help people enrich their careers?

The young woman above acknowledged that her age group has a less-than-ideal reputation, yet she feels that the stereotypes don't apply to her. Despite her view that she's not a typical Millennial, she still finds herself as a target for those with a bone to pick with her generation. It is clear that negative generalizations are not helpful, can be hurtful, and can impede both team productivity and personal success. Yet they are often tossed around casually, as if they are universally true.

So how can members of the different generations see beyond the stereotypes and instead focus on the positive traits of each cohort to build more unity and cooperation? I embarked on a study to get a sense of what matters to the different generations in life and for their careers. I explored values, how they feel about their time working, their thoughts on success and their career.

The Baby Boomers will mostly have exited the workplace within the next ten years, and there are simply not enough Gen X members to take their place. As a result, it is highly likely that more people will be working with and for individuals who are younger than themselves, be they direct supervisors, business partners, customers, or clients.

The youngest generation on the radar, Generation Z, generally born after 1995 or 1996 (also referred to as Gen Z), is poised to alter the workplace for many years to come.

We can all be better prepared for this transition by developing a more in-depth understanding of each generation and discovering the best gifts and talents each group brings to the table.

CHAPTER ONE

What Do We Know About Generation Z?

Where did the label *Gen Z* originate? It turns out that an internet contest in 2012, sponsored by *USA Today*, invited people to participate in selecting the name of the generation coming after the Millennials. The name *Generation Z* was a natural next generation in the sequence to Generation X and Generation Y. Other suggestions included *post-Millennial, iGeneration, Plurals, Gen Wii, Digital Natives, Founders, Net Gen, Generation Text, Gen Tech, or Homeland Generation.*[2] Whatever you care to call them, they are currently the youngest generation in the workplace.

Who Are They?

The members of Gen Z who participated in this study were born after 1998 and have never known a world without the internet. Their parents are Millennials and Gen X, who seem to have more of a "go figure it out yourself" approach to their parenting as opposed to the "helicopter" stance of Baby Boomer parents.[3] Older siblings are likely to be the so-called "Boomerang Kids," the Gen Yers who ended up coming back home during the financial crises of 2000 and 2008. During those lean years, grandparents were also a part of many households. At the same time, Gen Z is familiar with non-traditional households, in which families are no longer based on stereotypical gender roles with the father as the primary wage earner.[4]

Most members of Gen Z are just starting college or their first post-college jobs. However, this cohort will soon be making its mark on the workplace. According to the U.S. Census Bureau, Gen Z makes up about 25% of the population,[5] and if they have not already, they will soon be surpassing the Millennials as the largest cohort. By 2022, when they have fully joined the workforce, they will bring considerable influence to bear in the marketplace.

Major Influences on Generation Z. What Shaped Them?

Major national and international events have helped mold the values and ideals of Generation Z. Early in their lives, members of Gen Z experienced:

- The September 11, 2001 (9/11) World Trade Center attacks
- Two bear markets in 2000 and 2008
- Families in financial crisis
- Implementation of the Affordable Care Act
- School shootings
- Ongoing racial and ethnic tensions
- Legalization of medical marijuana in a number of states
- The rise of twenty-something billionaire entrepreneurs
- Coming of age during the administration of our first African-American President
- Gay marriage becoming legal and commonplace[3]

For Gen Z, there was never a time when social media didn't exist, and they view life through their smartphones and tablets, sharing music, photos, news, and opinions as easily as they breathe and eat. Their capacity for processing large amounts of information is considerable. For this generation, answers to virtually any question are typically only a few clicks or taps away.

Knowledge is important to this cohort. More members of Gen Z are projected to attend and graduate from college than their Gen Y predecessors. In addition to formal education, Gen Z is adept at accessing information and self-teaching, based on vast stores of information available on the internet.[3]

Looking Ahead with Gen Z

More members of Gen Z are becoming adults, beginning to find their own way, and preparing to make an impact. What trends in society will shape the world during the Gen Z era?

Trends in the Workplace

Many trends are converging in the workplace all at once:

- An increase in hiring and wages as well as a decrease in benefits packages offered
- Increased opportunities for virtual employment and other flexible working arrangements
- The retirement of Baby Boomers and the rise of Millennials to management
- Greater impact of technology in positive (i.e., productivity) and negative (i.e., distractions) ways
- Employment opportunities in science, technology, and healthcare are on the rise, and manual or unskilled labor jobs are on the decline.[6]

The rise of the "gig economy" benefits employers by providing lower costs and greater talent availability, and benefits workers by offering greater control over their lives and their income. Through services such as Uber and Airbnb, more people will be able to supplement their income or make their entire living using personal assets. They will also be able to freelance through online marketplaces seeking specific talents.[7] Self-employment or "intrapreneurship" opportunities where Gen Z can define their own career paths within a company, in cooperation with a company or completely outside a traditional employer arrangement, will become more commonplace.

The turbulent world of their childhood helped many members of Gen Z to become self-aware, self-sufficient, inventive, objective-oriented, and practical. They tend to have the maturity and sense of social justice that comes with seeing such up-close and personal tragedies as 9/11 and the financial crises.

Since they are accustomed to instant access to information and feedback via their smartphones, they are acutely responsive to needs of which they become aware, and ready to look for solutions. They are looking forward to employment with a great sense of realism rather than optimism, with very little sense of entitlement, and a desire to contribute in significant ways. They tend to choose career paths that will ensure financial stability.[8]

Culture

Generation Z will have to adapt to a wide variety of societal changes over the next few decades.

By 2020, there will be approximately 5 billion internet users on 80 billion devices worldwide. This connectivity will encompass work, home, and surrounding environments, and turn them into a "seamless experience." Our lifestyle preferences will live in the cloud and move with us as we navigate the offline world. "Smart" (connected, customizable, sensing, and self-monitoring) services, solutions, and governance will be the norm.[9]

Innovators will come closer to developing cars with zero emissions and accidents, cities with zero carbon footprints, and factories with minimal environmental impact.[9]

Urban clusters such as the Boston/New York/Washington Eastern Seaboard will take on the characteristics of nations or states. Local governments will have great impact on a national and global scale in terms of purchasing power and influence.[9]

Deep socioeconomic change will be felt by the influence of such social trends as the aging population, the influx of new immigrants bringing their own customs and religions, and the emergence of a global middle class as an internet-connected community.[9]

The diversity that seemed to have troubled earlier generations is mostly a non-issue for Gen Z. Probably the last with a Caucasian majority, Gen Z is the most racially and ethnically diverse generation in the United States. Census data for the racial and ethnic makeup of Gen Z[4] (for those who select a category) indicates that:

• 55% are Caucasian

- 24% are Hispanic
- 14% are African-American
- 4% are Asian

They have grown up interacting with and cooperating with people from most racial, ethnic, religious, and sexual backgrounds. This exposure gives them a broader perspective. As such, acceptance of difference will be one less struggle for them as they assume their role as responsible citizens in the United States.

Politics

The verdict is still out on whether members of Generation Z will have higher or lower voter participation rates. What we do know is that while most of Gen Z cannot yet vote, they have enough experience with weighty domestic and international issues to know that voting is very important. Such issues as the Affordable Care Act, illegal immigration, gender identity, and the economy tend to be high priorities, and they view politicians with distrust, often expressing the opinion that the U.S. is not heading in the right direction.[10]

Given the general discontent with politicians and the growing concern that there has been little or no progress on major issues of societal need, perhaps Gen Z will be seeking more transparency, action, and accountability when they begin voting in the next few election cycles. These expectations will also most likely influence their assessment of leaders in other parts of their life.

Generation Z in the Workplace

The following chapters take a look at a few specific characteristics of Gen Z. Each one will conclude with practical tips for Gen Z workers as they pursue job success and for supervisors as they assimilate members of Gen Z into their teams.

Let's examine Gen Z Values, Goals, Workplace Preferences, and Attitudes.

CHAPTER TWO

Values

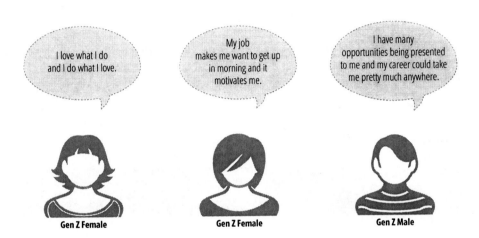

Values are principles or standards of behavior that one holds to be important. Our values shape the way we think about what's going on in the world, the words we use to express ourselves, and the ways we act in different circumstances. When we make decisions, we are generally guided in one direction or another by our values.

What does Gen Z hold to be important, both professionally and personally? What impact might these values have on the workplace as Gen Z becomes a larger part of the workforce?

What Does Gen Z Value?

Professional and personal values shape our priorities and how we manifest them. In this chapter, we take a look at what Gen Z values. The way these young workers show up in the workplace will eventually have a larger impact on the society as a whole.

Two key topics examined in my study were personal and professional values. In order to understand what motivates individuals, it is helpful to understand what they want out of life and which pursuits they will put energy toward.

Overview of Gen Z Personal Values

Taking a look at personal values, the survey asked: *What is most important to you in your life right now from a personal perspective?*

I asked the participants to rank six concepts—*career, relationships with family and friends, financial security, faith, health, and relationships*—in order of importance to them.

For Gen Z, *happiness* was the most important to the respondents as a group, followed by *relationships with family and friends, health, financial security, career,* and *faith.* Gen Z ranked *happiness* significantly higher than did the Baby Boomers and Gen X.

Gen Z Ranking for Personal Values in Order of Importance
1. Happiness
2. Relationships
3. Health
4. Financial Security
5. Career
6. Faith

Men ranked *happiness* and *relationships* as the top two values; women agreed on the top two but ranked *relationships* over *happiness.*

Gen Z Ranking for Personal Values in Order of Importance by Gender	
Men	**Women**
1. Happiness	1. Relationships
2. Relationships	2. Happiness
3. Career	3. Health
4. Health	4. Financial Security
5. Financial Security	5. Career
6. Faith	6. Faith

Financial security, while important, ranked below many other values. This is not terribly surprising, as all four cohorts have lived through several seismic economic shifts, which may lead some to be more reflective on what really matters in life.

As with the concept of *happiness*, Gen Z ranked *faith* significantly higher than both Gen X and the Baby Boomers. *Happiness* and *faith* were left to individual interpretation, however, so this particular result could be a function of the optimism of the younger generation that is just starting out. They tend to exhibit hope and confidence in the quality and accessibility of opportunities available for chasing one's dreams.

Gen Z ranked *career* nearly last of the six values, and overall, they ranked *career* lower than did the other generation cohorts.

Overview of Gen Z Professional Values

Gen Z members acknowledge the importance of financial security and value the satisfaction of a job well done, but they are unwilling to sacrifice a personal life on the altar of career success.

Regarding professional values, I asked: *What is important to you professionally right now?*

The Gen Z respondents ranked the following six value concepts in order of importance: *doing well in current role, making more money, work-life balance, promotion, changing career,* and *retirement.*

Gen Z Ranking for Professional Values in Order of Importance
1. Doing Well in Role
2. Making More Money
3. Work-life Balance
4. Promotion
5. Changing Career
6. Retirement

Doing well in current role and *making more money* tied for the top spot in the ranking. The implication of these top two rankings may be that financial incentives are as important to Gen Z as job satisfaction. Other incentives such as gaining experience or developing new skills, while valuable, may be less appealing to them.

I did observe some interesting differences by gender. With respect to the top two personal values, the men and women had a reversed order; male Gen Zers listed *making more money* as most important, and the female Gen Zers listed *doing well in current role* as most important.

Gen Z Ranking for Professional Values in Order of Importance by Gender	
Men	**Women**
1. Making More Money	1. Doing Well in Role
2. Doing Well in Role	2. Making More Money
3. Work-life Balance	3. Work-life Balance
4. Getting a Promotion	4. Getting a Promotion
5. Changing Career	5. Changing Career
6. Retirement	6. Retirement

My study found that money is less important to Gen Z than it is to the older cohorts. Instead, Gen Z prefers opportunity to advance over making more money as a motivator in the workplace. At the same time, 16% of Gen Z in my study reported they would also like to start their own businesses and be the boss. Another human resources study reported that one in five Gen Zers would like to telecommute rather than occupy a traditional workspace.[11]

Work-life balance ranked after *making more money* and *doing well in current role*, and was considered more important than *promotion*. This is reflective of other feedback in the study, which indicates that members of Gen Z, while fully committed to financial and job success, still largely value "having a life."

Perhaps because they are just starting out, *changing career* is not a major concern. Likewise, *retirement* is not a high priority for Gen Z.

Gen Z and the American Dream

Gen Z Male

Gen Z Female

Central to the values discussion is the framing of opportunity for Americans through the concept of the American Dream. This ideal was famously described by James Truslow Adams in 1931, who stated that "life should be better and richer and fuller for everyone, with opportunity for each according to ability or achievement," not impeded by social rank, circumstances of birth, or other similar barriers.[12]

Pursuit of education and home ownership have generally been seen as the benchmarks of the American Dream, while different generations and different economic trends have squeezed other facets into or out of the broader understanding of the concept over the years. As a national ethos, it implies the virtues and rewards of hard work and determination.

Many Americans have expressed concern that the traditional American Dream may no longer be representative of what the average American can truly attain. By and large, they point to the economic reality that many households have trouble just paying the bills on a monthly basis, and have no possibility of saving for higher education or buying a house. Other people have been content to adjust their concept of the American Dream to encompass personal fulfillment and attainment of their own set of ideals.

To better understand Gen Z's perceptions of the American Dream, I asked the study participants to rank six concepts based on how important they are to their vision of the American Dream. They ranked the concepts in this order: *being able to achieve goals, financial security, ability to pursue education, freedom of speech, building a legacy, and home ownership.*

The Vast Majority of Gen Z Believe in the American Dream

When the members of Gen Z were asked if they believe that their version of the American Dream is achievable, an overwhelming 95% said YES! This level of optimism is higher than that of the average American in my study.

Overall, 87% of Americans in my study still believe the American Dream is achievable. The other three cohorts are less optimistic than the national average, with the Baby Boomer at 80%, Gen X at 83%, and Gen Y at 88%.

Gen Z Ranking for the American Dream in Order of Importance
1. Being Able to Achieve Goals
2. Financial Security
3. Ability to Pursue Education
4. Freedom of Speech
5. Building a Legacy
6. Home Ownership

While Gen Z male and female respondents both listed *being able to achieve goals* as the most important element of the American Dream, the rankings diverged significantly after that. As shown in the table below, males chose this order: *financial security, freedom of speech, pursuit of education, building a legacy, home ownership*, while the females selected this order: *education, finances, freedom of speech, home ownership, and legacy.*

Gen Z Ranking for the American Dream in Order of Importance by Gender	
Men	Women
1. Being Able to Achieve Goals	1. Being Able to Achieve Goals
2. Financial Security	2. Ability to Pursue Education
3. Freedom of Speech	3. Financial Security
4. Ability to Pursue Education	4. Freedom of Speech
5. Building a Legacy	5. Home Ownership
6. Home Ownership	6. Building a Legacy

Reasons Why Gen Z Does Not Believe in the American Dream

I don't believe the American Dream is achievable to me because I don't come from money, and while college can help me get a well paying job, the idea of student debt terrifies me.

Gen Z Female

The American Dream is an illusive phrase used to mislead many Americans. I am a woman. I do not think I will have the same opportunities with the American Dream.

Gen Z Female

When the Gen Z participants indicated they felt that the American Dream was not achievable, I asked them to share a reason. The most common response was that financial challenges such as the cost of college and not being able to get a job due to the state of the economy were insurmountable. Some respondents doubted the validity of the American Dream as a legitimate pursuit.

The top three reasons why Gen Z didn't believe in the ideal of the American Dream were:

- They cannot afford to get a college education.
- Fear that they will not be able to get a job
- The dream isn't realistic for modern times.

Implications for Working Relationships and Career Paths

Job satisfaction usually comes down to day-to-day interactions and accomplishments. Sometimes the vaguest perceptions can become points of conflict over the simplest differences in thinking and priorities.

Consider the following statements:

My boss is on this kick about structuring the breaks differently and giving us more flexibility when we have to be in to the office. She wants all this input from us and keeps changing our schedules to try to see what works best. What works best? Let me do my work. Why are you worried about the times we're working? Just tell me what you want and let me do it right. – Gen Z Male

I'm trying to improve office morale by letting the employees pick schedules that suit their own work styles a little more, but I've got a few kids that seem to think it's just stupid. I'd have thought they'd want the flexibility the most, so they can answer all their important little messages all day and stay in touch. They just don't appreciate the efforts I'm putting in here. – Gen X Female

In this case, both people want a good outcome. But they have different perspectives on what is important. In cases such as these, it's helpful to be open-minded and willing to accept the other person's point of view. Open and interactive communication can be one of the best ways to bring about understanding and reduce frustration and misunderstanding.

Practical Suggestions for Gen Z Employees

Remember that your boss is probably trying to relate to you and provide you with a more satisfactory workplace without necessarily understanding your priorities.

- **Seek to understand what's important.** While your manager's priorities seem very different from yours, try to find out what their goals are to help you address them.
- **Share what's on your mind.** You can also try to express your own point of view so others can see where you're coming from.
- **Be positive and constructive.** Remember, your goal is to perform well and be productive. You can help the whole team move forward well by participating with a positive mindset, even if the objective or way of getting a task accomplished might not be important to you personally.
- **There are multiple paths to a college education.** One of the great things about America is that where you start does not have to dictate where you can go in your life or where you will end up. Many Americans believe that education is the key to success. However, with rising college costs, affordability can be a challenge for some. You may want to consider alternatives to pursuing the traditional path of attending a four-year college right after high school. Some of your options beyond student loans include:
  - Community college
  - Military service
  - Trade school
  - Studying overseas
  - Paying as you go
  - Broad array of scholarships and grants

- **Having patience is key.** The American Dream is alive and well. Remember that you're in this career journey for the long haul at this point, and everything you do now will be part of the foundation of the life you want to achieve.
- **Be prepared to work hard to put yourself in the best position to get what you want.** Make sure that your values guide your decisions and that you don't undermine yourself with choices that ultimately lead where you don't want to go.

Questions to Ask Your Supervisor
What are your expectations for me in this role?   • Will I have to work overtime, on weekends?   • What is the dress code?   • How do you like to receive information (e.g., email, face-to-face, or instant message)?
Notes:
What does it take to be successful in this job and at this organization/ company?   • How did you get to where you are?   • What are career-limiting moves that I should avoid?
Notes:

Exercise 1
Preparing for Success

List questions you will ask your supervisor about how to be successful in your current role?
1.
2.
3.

Practical Suggestions for Gen Z Supervisors

Your Gen Z worker's aspirations are likely very similar to goals that you envisioned and pursued at one time.

- **Teach the basics.** Perhaps you entered the workplace when the expectation was that you had to figure things out on your own. It was a rite of passage. However, today swift answers to any question are a quick internet search away. Think of ways to encourage the practical aspects of career advancement, like good work habits and skills that will serve them well in any job.

- **Show them the money.** Remember that your Gen Z employee most likely values making more money and doing well in her role over the other perks you are offering. Frequently remind them about the connection between their performance and the rewards they can expect, such as promotions, recognition, bonuses, and premium shifts. If you can frame your offering or request in terms of how it adds to your Gen Z employee's success or financial security, they will more likely participate and add to the value of what you're trying to establish for the team or organization.

Questions for Supervisors of Gen Z to Consider
Can you accept that historical and economic events mean that modern workers have different expectations than workers who entered the work-force even a generation ago?
Notes:

Questions for Supervisors of Gen Z to Consider

Have you shared what good performance looks like?

Notes:

Have you created an environment where questions can be asked and answered?

Notes:

CHAPTER THREE

Goals

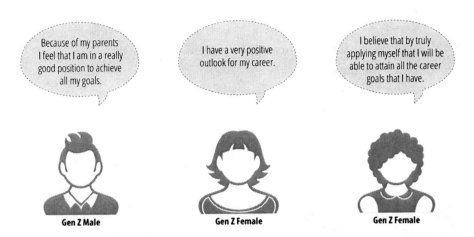

Because of my parents I feel that I am in a really good position to achieve all my goals.

Gen Z Male

I have a very positive outlook for my career.

Gen Z Female

I believe that by truly applying myself that I will be able to attain all the career goals that I have.

Gen Z Female

Two of the common frustrations I've heard from managers throughout my research about younger workers are that they will not stay at one place very long and they cannot invest fully in their job. Additionally, the experiences of older workers with shrinking job availability tend to dampen personal optimism when it comes to career outlook, and these doubts are often projected onto our younger workforce members.

What are members of Gen Z looking for career-wise when they look ahead with their longer-term goals in mind? Having grown up seeing their Gen X parents and some Gen Y siblings struggle through bear markets, they understand that any career plan has to factor in the possibility of economic downturns. Where do they feel they are in relation to where they want to eventually be in their careers?

How Does Gen Z Feel about Their Career Opportunities?

As part of my research, I asked the Gen Z respondents two questions and gave them the opportunity to explain their answers.

The first question: *How do you rate your current career opportunities?* The rating options were *excellent, good, average, poor,* and *awful.*

The majority of the respondents had favorable views of their career options.

- 66% of the Gen Z participants (69% of males and 61% of females) rated their career opportunities as *good* or *excellent*
- 34% of the males rated their career opportunities as *excellent*
- 21% of females thought their career prospects were *excellent*
- 27% of Gen Z are expecting *excellent* opportunities

This optimistic view so early on in their career, set against the backdrop of a recovering economy, is encouraging.

Gen Z Rating of Their Career Opportunities by Gender		
	Men	**Women**
Average	25%	35%
Awful	0%	1%
Excellent	0%	21%
Good	34%	40%
Poor	6%	3%

What Makes Career Options Excellent for Gen Z?

Respondents were then asked to explain their answer. The primary reason that many of them viewed their career prospects as *excellent* was the availability of opportunities for career growth. The second most popular reason cited was love for their current job. The third reason mentioned was good pay and flexible working terms.

Job satisfaction is high. This type of response constituted 15% of the replies. The respondents' free-form explanations for their optimistic outlooks included comments such as:

- *"I love my job"*
- *"Because the environment I work in is amazing"*
- *"My job is great"*
- *"I love what I do and do what I love"*

Lots of opportunity. Approximately 9% of the responses revolved around abundant opportunities in their field

Hard work and planning pays off. Another 9% of the Gen Z respondents identified recognition that their own hard work and planning impacted their career outlook.

Money matters. Four percent of those identifying their career prospects as *excellent* mentioned good pay as the reason.

These responses are in line with the notion that members of Gen Z value doing well in their role, being able to contribute meaningfully to their workplaces, and making good money. The abundance of options makes it more likely that members of Gen Z will be able to find something they can do well and be paid well for their work.

As a group, 31% reported *average* prospects and only 4% thought their current career opportunities were *poor* or *awful.* One respondent stated that the company was treating employees horribly, which led her to see her career opportunities as *poor.* This response demonstrates that management can play a key role in shaping how employees view their long-term career prospects within the organization.

What Makes a Job Ideal for Gen Z?

The next question was: *Are you in your ideal job for this stage in your life?* The answers to choose from were *definitely not, probably not, maybe, probably yes, and definitely yes.*

The Gen Z respondents generally had high expectations for their careers and felt that they were on the right track—a positive attitude that should be valued and supported. The study results showed that:

- 64% of participants liked their current outlook
- 59% thought they were where they needed to be at the moment

Roughly the same proportions who indicated *definitely yes* and *probably yes* had also selected *excellent* and *good* for their career prospects. While studies show that most people will change jobs five or more times throughout their career, my study suggests that Gen Z appear to be thoughtful about early career choices.

The male and female participants responded with roughly similar numbers regarding what they thought of their career opportunities. Sixty-five percent of men and 56% of women thought they were *definitely* or *probably* in their ideal jobs; 29% of males and 19% of females reported that they were *definitely* in their ideal jobs.

Gen Z Views on Being in Ideal Job by Gender		
	Men	**Women**
Definitely Yes	29%	19%
Probably Yes	36%	37%
Maybe	12%	9%
Probably Not	17%	22%
Definitely Not	6%	13%

The reasons given for the remaining responses of *maybe, probably not,* and *definitely not* suggest that the Gen Z respondents had a good idea of what they wanted out of their careers. In order of how frequently each answer was given, the top responses were:

- Current job is only temporary while at school for intended trade or career goal
- Not what Gen Z intends to do or wanted to do long-term
- Job was not in their field of expertise so their skills were not being used to fullest
- Job is not paying well

• No room for career growth
• Want to move up to something better
• No enjoyment in the current job
• Mental health is being negatively impacted by the job

Many respondents viewed their current jobs as temporary. The majority of those who had plans other than their current jobs were in school or training. This corresponds with the numbers that show that Gen Z is stacking up to be the most highly educated cohort ever.

Those who stated that they didn't intend to stay in their current jobs long-term indicated that they had clear goals in mind and were biding their time until something better came along. This corresponds with the idea that Gen Z is practical and realistic about how advancement is achieved and how important financial security is for their lives and careers.

Later chapters will discuss those Gen Z workers who are determined to forge long-term relationships with their employers (see Chapter Four – Work Environment Preferences).

Implications for Working Relationships and Career Paths

Members of Gen Z come to the workplace with a positive outlook on career possibilities and high expectations of themselves in terms of creating their own success. Many of these workers just starting out find themselves in excellent positions and express the desire to stay more than just a year or two. This bodes well for both the employee and the employer.

Consider the following statements:

I love my job and I can really envision myself staying here for a long time. My manager, however, keeps trying to pull me back, telling me there's no room for moving up right now. Or, he tells me to be patient and take time to learn more. I don't think he appreciates me.
– Gen Z Female

I have these great kids come in here who do great work, but it makes me nervous when they broach the subject of promotions. It's a small department. There's nowhere to let them go that won't step on someone else's toes. They are going to have to wait until an opportunity opens up and that could take time. I try to explain this, but it seems to fall on deaf ears. I don't want to lose them, because they are so good for the company. Inevitably, I fear that they will quit on me. – Baby Boomer Male

I worked hard in college. I had great internships and I'm a quick learner. I've been doing this job for almost a year and I can do it in my sleep. I'm ready for more. I just don't understand why I am not getting a promotion. – Gen Z Male

It boggles my mind that these young workers think that just because they have a degree that it is an instant substitute for experience. Doing something once doesn't mean you've mastered it. Actually knowing what you are doing through hard-earned experience matters. – Gen X Female

Being optimistic about your choices and circumstances is helpful. It can provide better focus and help you navigate the eventful challenges that are inherent in every job. That said, experience is also a good teacher; not all things can be taught or learned in books or in a classroom.

Practical Suggestions for Gen Z Employees

If you're in a good place right now in terms of your career goals, good! If not, that's fine too.

- **Learn all you can.** Take advantage of every opportunity to learn and grow, even if it's only sideways growth for a while.
- **Lateral moves are fine.** Keep in mind that your best next step may take you to another employer or to school, if your current employer does not have the need or the ability to take full advantage of your skills and desire to contribute.
- **Stay positive.** Remember that all is not lost if you're in a less than ideal job now. It's a waste of time only if you decide it isn't worth

your time. Do your best where you are and keep an open mind as you explore what you want in terms of long-term goals.

- **Many jobs require some type of training or formal education.** Formal education may or may not be part of your next step, but plan to make some kind of investment in training so that you can move up when you know what you really want to do. More advanced skills will open the doors to career advancement opportunities and better money. You'll just have to pay some dues to get there.

Questions to Ask Yourself

What is really important in your job or career right now?
- Money?
- Commute time?
- Job growth?

Notes:

How well equipped are you to achieve your goals?
- What skills do you have or need to learn?
- Are you ready to work hard to achieve your goals?

Notes:

Questions to Ask Yourself
How well equipped are you to achieve your goals? • What skills do you have or need to learn? • Are you ready to work hard to achieve your goals
Notes:

Exercise 2
Setting Priorities

List the top three things that will be important for you—personally and/or professionally—in the next six to 12 months and then have at least two conversations with someone you trust about how you accomplish these goals.

1.

2.

3.

Practical Suggestions for Gen Z Supervisors

Many employees join with the goal of staying for the long haul, and they want a company that they can grow with over time. Making a commitment to help Gen Z workers develop and grow in the organization will help them stay engaged in the company's day-to-day success over the long term.

Realize that your young workers might be a little impatient and eager to try something new after only a short time.

- **Let them know that they are valued.** Give your Gen Z workers the opportunity to grow and advance as far as possible, utilizing their technology prowess and desire to contribute, while making sure they know they are important to the success of the company.
- **Be clear about the next steps.** While most workers today change jobs more than five times throughout their career, some prefer to stick with one company, or they may leave and then return to the same company at a later stage in their career. In any case, your management style and support of their development and their ability to achieve their goals will play a huge role in their decision to stay or go.
- **If promotions are not available, make sure growth is an option.** Manage expectations by being transparent regarding the path toward greater opportunities and growth. You can best prepare them for their next step by encouraging them to learn as much as they can and grow where they are.
- **Gen Z is pragmatic and not shy about moving on.** Be prepared for them to move on when their goals outstrip what you can offer them, and send them off with goodwill and positive encouragement.

Questions for Supervisors of Gen Z to Consider

Have you spent time sharing what a career at your company can look like for your employees?

Notes:

Does your employee have a realistic development plan?

Notes:

Questions for Supervisors of Gen Z to Consider

How well do you represent your organization?

Notes:

Do your actions motivate employees to stay or leave?

Notes:

CHAPTER FOUR

Work Environment Preferences

Do what you want to do. Don't let others tell you what they want you to do because it isn't their life. You follow your dreams.

Either fully commit to what you are doing right now or change everything.

Never take the bottom dollar and make it your goal. Have more confidence in your abilities and strive for the top

Do a great job and you will move up in your work.

Gen Z Female   **Gen Z Female**   **Gen Z Female**   **Gen Z Male**

Members of Gen Z in the workforce are mostly around 20 years old, just getting started. What is the workplace they are stepping into? What are they looking for?

Recent surveys have a lot to say about significant trends in the American workplace that are having widespread impact. Gen Z will have a unique perspective on workplace norms. They don't have a sense of history about how workplaces used to be. But they do have their preferences, in terms of their idea of an ideal job, and in terms of an ideal supervisor.

Recent Changes in the American Workplace

Information and Technology

Above all, technology has created widespread change in the work environment, including how and when and where we work. The past

decade has been witness to broader acceptance and use of full- or part-
time remote employment, which was facilitated by advances in electronic
networking, videoconferencing, and the accessibility of virtually all types
of information. According to the U.S. Bureau of Labor Statistics, in 2015,
about 24% of workers did some or all of their work from home.[13] Flex-
time, creative work spaces, and outsourcing have impacted daily work,
and there are more resources available in terms of in-house services to
enhance the health and productivity of employees.[14]

Gen Z Female

Gen Z Female

Gen Z Male

Use of technology presents perhaps the clearest demarcations between
the generations. Baby Boomers prefer face-to-face; Gen X reaches for the
phone; Gen Z like their social media and emails. Gen Z likes messaging
apps where communications are quick and then gone, no "paper trail." Gen
Z is saturated in social media and internet access, and is more accepting
of smartphones as banks and tools for social interactions. The younger
generations also are more likely than their elder cohorts to request or take
advantage of work-from-home arrangements.[15]

Members of Gen Z, more than their predecessors, have mastered
existence in the virtual world, where they see themselves as influencers, able
to persuade, attract attention, and achieve celebrity status. However, one
interesting finding reported is that while Gen Z has grown up with more
technology than any other cohort, and they like to work with technology
to attain their work goals, 51% prefer face-to-face communication with
their supervisors and coworkers. One study showed that nearly 36% of

Gen Z survey respondents acknowledged that instant messaging was the biggest work-time distraction.[15]

Diversity

At the same time that technology is increasing productivity, there is increased diversity in age and background of coworkers. Reflective of this, Americans believe that it takes both technical and social savvy to navigate the workplace successfully. Competence with computers and being able to work with people from widely diverse backgrounds rank as most important, ahead of training in writing, communication, math, and science.[6]

U.S. employment trends point to increasing demand for advanced education, training, and experience for a wider range of industries, and a decline in need for physical and manual skill. Education and healthcare are seeing the greatest industry growth, helping to create this need for greater education and training. Fifty-four percent of workers, representing all education levels, see that their future success in staying abreast of changes in the workplace will involve continuing skill development, predominantly in further formal education. Young adults are particularly aware of this, likely due in large part to the length of the working tenure ahead of them.[6]

Pay

Pay has not been increasing in step with expenses and, if available at all, the benefits packages offered by employers have been shrinking in scope and value. At the same time, the average workweek length has increased to 38.6 hours, and Americans are taking less time off, clocking an average of nearly 46 weeks per year. Length of job tenure is on the rise, with just over half of workers staying with current employers for five-plus years, as opposed to 46% staying that long ten years ago.[6]

Given that we spend so much of our time working both in and out of the office, the work environment can play a crucial role in how we perform.

Generation Z in the American Workplace

Gen Z may be new to the whole working scene, and they, as with all previous generations, come with their own quirks and preferences. What are they bringing to the American workplace?

Education

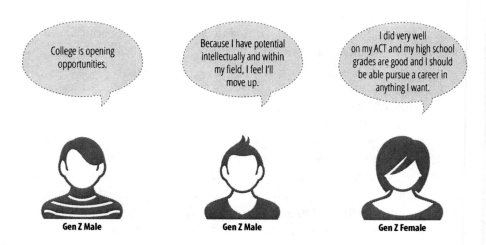

College is opening opportunities.

Because I have potential intellectually and within my field, I feel I'll move up.

I did very well on my ACT and my high school grades are good and I should be able pursue a career in anything I want.

Gen Z Male   Gen Z Male   Gen Z Female

Nearly 18% of the Gen Z members in my sample reported only high school education or less, and 62% reported some college education or at least an Associate's degree. Only 6% reported a Bachelor's degree or some graduate work. These numbers align with other findings and make sense based on assumptions that these young adult workers are still pursuing education.

What are the current trends regarding higher education? Following an increase of 36% in undergraduate enrollment in degree-granting post-secondary schools from 2000 to 2010, the National Center for Education Statistics reported that enrollment dropped by 4% between 2010 and 2014. An uptick has begun again, and enrollment is projected to increase by 14% by the year 2025.[16]

Another study reports that Gen Z views higher education to be of the utmost importance, believing that it will be the best means of preparing for a good job. According to the study, 82% of the Gen Z respondents are intending to head to college immediately after high school, and even if they are not sure which school it will be, most have a good idea of what type of school. About 66% of those surveyed plan to attend a four-year school, while 20% are considering a technical or trade program.[17]

Gen Z and Work Preferences

Although the stereotypes persist, members of Gen Z are not a bunch of slackers. While nearly 6% of Gen Z respondents in my study reported that they weren't currently employed, none of them stated that they would prefer not working.

My study found that nearly 80% the Gen Z labor force is willing to work and available for half- to full-time jobs. Only 16% of those working fewer than 20 hours a week said that this was ideal for them. The highest percentage of Gen Z employees both do work and want to work 21-40 hours per week, 46% and 53% respectively.

How Many Hours Per Week Would Gen Z Like to Work?	
Under 20 hours	17%
21-40 hours	53%
41-50 hours	18%
51-60 hours	8%
60+ hours	4%

As a group, 30% (19% of Gen Z men and 14% of Gen Z women) would like to work 40 or more hours per week. Members of Gen Z are willing and able to put in a reasonable workweek and will infuse America's workforce with educated and tech-savvy professionals.

Gen Z Views on Being in Ideal Job by Gender		
	Men	Women
Under 20 hours	15%	18%
21-40 hours	46%	57%
41-50 hours	23%	15%
51-60 hours	11%	7%
60+ hours	5%	3%

Gen Z and Ideal Job Tenure

Given that changing jobs is now a common occurrence, it has been suggested that some employers are reluctant to invest in young talent. They fear that they are just getting a talented worker ready for their next employer. Does the investment in the newest members of the workforce make sense? Yes.

How Long Do Gen Z Workers Plan to Stay with Their Current Employer?	
Less Than 1 Year	15%
1-2 Years	32%
3-5 Years	31%
6-10 Years	8%
10+ Years	14%

Members of Gen Z tend to show up with a plan to stay. In my study, most of the Gen Z respondents (63%) plan to remain at their current employer for 1-5 years, roughly half for 1-2, and half for 3-5 years. Eight percent indicated intentions of staying at their current place of employment for 6-10 years and about 14% intend to stay ten or more years.

How Long Do Gen Z Workers Plan to Stay with Their Current Employer, by Gender?		
	Men	**Women**
1-2 Years	31%	33%
10+ Years	22%	10%
3-5 Years	34%	30%
6-10 Years	7%	8%
Less Than 1 Year	6%	19%

Twenty-nine percent of Gen Z men and 18% of Gen Z women indicated that they would like to stay with their current employer for 6 or more years. This is in contrast to the national average job tenure of 4.2 years for wage and salary workers.[18] Investing in a Gen Z employee would certainly seem worthwhile if they stick around for 6 years or longer.

What % of Gen Z Workers Plan to Stay on the Job More Than Six Years, by Gender?	
Men	**Women**
29%	18%

Of the Gen Z respondents, 15% stated intentions of staying with their current employer for less than 1 year. Several reasons were given for this. Ranked from the most frequent to the least frequent responses, the reasons for leaving their current jobs in less than a year were:

- Looking for better career opportunities and situations
- Relocating
- Pursuing education
- This was a temporary job rather than a career situation
- No passion for current position
- Low pay
- Obligations to other priorities
- Fear that the company would be going out of business

Relocating, with no other explanation, could fall under pursuit of education, finishing their education, or viewing the job as a temporary position and not a career. These top answers suggest that members of Generation Z are carefully planning their careers based on thoughtful educational and career path choices.

Gen Z and the Boss

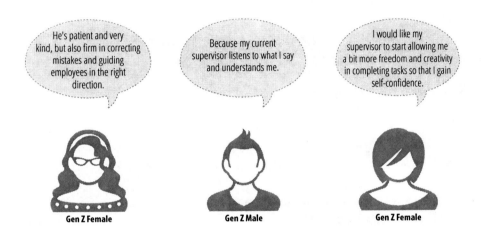

Most jobs these days require high levels of leadership and com-munication skill in order to successfully coordinate teams and projects. Flexibility and willingness to try new things are critical. Supervisors are in key positions to teach their younger employees these crucial skills.[19]

Some studies show that most Gen Z workers (61%) want their supervisors to listen to their ideas and give their contributions equal time, and 65% of Gen Z workers also say that their coworkers and supervisors can enable their best work.[15] These observations are consistent with my findings.

Factors Influencing Creative Work Environments

There are many factors that influence creative and innovative work environments, such as:

• Support for an "outside the box" approach

- Sufficient time for producing novel work
- The availability of training
- Management practices that allow freedom or autonomy at work
- Provision of challenging, interesting work
- Specification of clear overall strategic goals
- Formation of work teams by drawing together individuals with diverse skills and perspectives[20]

In this book, I wanted to focus on how certain management practices can influence the Gen Z journey at work.

How Gen Z Feels about Their Boss

Study participants had the opportunity to rate their current supervisor as a leader using *excellent, good, average, poor,* or *awful.* Compared to the other generational cohorts in the study, more Gen Z members indicated that their boss was an excellent or good leader.

Eighty-four percent of Gen Z participants considered their boss an *excellent* or *good* leader; 36% of respondents rated their boss *excellent* as a leader, and 48% rated the boss as *good* as a leader. The remaining 16% selected *average, poor, or awful* to describe their boss.

Gen Z Rating of Their Boss as a Leader	
Excellent	36%
Good	48%
Average	9%
Poor	6%
Awful	1%

Along with their rating, participants were asked to explain their selections. There were many reasons given for an *excellent* boss rating, ranging from personality to leadership skills.

Some Gen Z respondents mentioned personal attributes that they appreciated, such as:

- *Listening*
- *Understanding*
- *Helpfulness*
- *Organization*
- *Caring*
- *Ability to teach*
- *Balancing work and jokes*
- *Calmness*
- *Fairness*
- *Vision*
- *Easygoing manner*
- *Patience*
- *Good communication*
- *Friendliness*
- *Respectfulness*
- *Taking the time to get to know people*

Good leadership qualities specifically mentioned include: firm but kind guidance in correcting mistakes and redirecting expectations, pushing workers to do their best, adequate training, good direct feedback, knowing what everyone is doing, and getting everyone to work together.

Gen Z Male   Gen Z Male   Gen Z Female   Gen Z Male

In my study, Gen Z respondents gave specific feedback as to what their supervisors could do that they felt would help them to succeed in their current role. Respondents were given the opportunity to answer these two questions: *1) Please list one thing you would like your supervisor to START doing to help you be more successful in your role; and 2) Please list one thing you would like your supervisor to STOP doing to help you be more successful in your role.*

Nearly 12% said that there was nothing they could ask their supervisor to start or stop doing that would increase their chances of job success, which suggests a general sense of comfort with the approach and style of their current manager.

What Does Gen Z Want Their Bosses to Start Doing?

Gen Z respondents shared lots of feedback on how their managers can help them be more successful in their roles. Below are the most common responses:

- *"Provide opportunity and encouragement and freedom to take initiative and move ahead"*
- *"Give clear and detailed communications about directions and expectations"*
- *"Offer more feedback on things well done"*
- *"Ensure better hours and resolve scheduling issues"*
- *"Secure better pay and benefits"*
- *"Offer appropriate and continuing training, including cross-training in other departments"*
- *"In general, be a boss who is kinder, respectful, supportive, and understanding."*

What Does Gen Z Want Their Bosses to Stop Doing?

Gen Z participants had a long list of things that they would like their bosses to stop doing in order to help them be more successful. Below are the top responses:

- "Nagging"
- "Complaining"
- "Yelling"
- "Being rude or harsh"
- "Micromanaging"
- "Being vague"
- "Playing favoritism"
- "Not being available"
- "Showing a lack of trust"
- "Worrying about their youth"
- "Treating them like children"

Implications for Working Relationships and Career Paths

Gen Z is ready and willing to work. Contrary to popular opinions about the youngest workers just out of high school, they are not necessarily lacking in ambition. Yes, they are young and may be less mature than their more tenured coworkers. They may lack experience and have less than ideal work habits; however, most have a good handle on what it will take to succeed in their current jobs.

Some of them know they will not be staying long in their current roles, either because of their own life plans or the fact that the organization is a poor fit for them. A significant portion of Gen Z members, however, seem willing and able to commit to their current employment for the time being and for the foreseeable future.

Most members of Gen Z want to be fully engaged in work they enjoy. They want to expand their experience and get ahead in their careers. Of the reasons cited for intending to leave their jobs within a year, the majority stated that they were looking for better career opportunities and situations.

Gen Z is absolutely ready to contribute and lead in terms of applying technology for everyday work functions and ongoing improvements. This includes changes that are rapidly expanding employment options in healthcare and education. They can easily keep pace with the demands of school and work.

They want a boss they can respect. Overwhelmingly, Gen Z recognizes and appreciates positive interpersonal qualities such as kindness, respectfulness, friendliness, and an easygoing personality. They also value leadership that exhibits fairness, flexibility, receptivity to employee input, a willingness to teach, and an ability to support the success of the entire team. Yet, they may be receiving mixed messages from their peers, coworkers, and supervisors.

Consider the following statements:

This boss thinks I'm such a goof-off and always shuts me up when I try to mention something that could help out—I mean we don't even have VOIP yet. That old system is such ancient trash! I get my work done and then he gets so mad when he catches me looking at new systems that could pull the whole company out of the stone ages. I'm trying to explain this and he's lecturing at me about a poor work ethic. – Gen Z Male

The lady manager in our department treats me like an infant. She gets so impatient when I ask questions, but jeez, I've been here four months and I'm supposed to know what the supervisors know? I try to search the electronic files for answers, but they don't exist. Yeah, I don't know what I'm doing—she won't tell me! She's a rotten manager, if you ask me. – Gen Z Female

One of my new guys is such a smart-mouth, always slacking off and then trying to tell me how to do my job. If he was that smart, he'd be asking for more work, not wasting company time drooling over and complaining about electronics we'll never have the budget for anyway. He's not going far with that kind of attitude.
– Baby Boomer Male

I really try not to hire anyone under age 25 if I can help it at all. Compared to my older staff, they don't know anything and they don't take any initiative to learn anything more than they already know. – Gen X Male

The statements above demonstrate that we all enter the workforce with our life experiences and unique points of view. However, if we take time to understand another person's perspective, we allow ourselves the opportunity to grow, broaden our thinking, and perhaps even change our minds.

Practical Suggestions for Gen Z Employees

Your supervisor might be unconsciously reacting to your youth and inexperience by subjecting you to the same expectations as the more tenured or experienced workers.

- **Managers are human too.** Remember that your boss might be frustrated or intimidated by what you know and feel threatened by change that is easy for you. There might also be other circumstances that prevent him from taking your advice, like lack of funds or other needed support in the company. Or, they may not prioritize the value of efficiency over getting work done in the established way.

- **Choose to be assertive rather than aggressive.** Feeling that you are not being heard can be frustrating. However, if the person you are trying to communicate with feels threatened, they may be become defensive and the conversation may not be constructive. Try to find low-key or non-threatening ways to introduce your ideas to others who might be able to help bring about positive change in the organization.

- **Sometimes you have to compromise.** You may also have to just accept conditions as they are and develop a plan to succeed with the tools available to you. Compromise does not have to mean losing; perhaps you can find middle ground.

- **Raise your hand.** If you feel like you're being overlooked and discounted because you don't know everything yet, try asking for feedback and more responsibilities. Perhaps a respected, more experienced coworker can give you some feedback about how you're doing work-wise and how you might improve.

- **You have to prove yourself.** Start by performing the tasks you're given as well as you can. If you're frustrated with poor instruction and unspoken expectations, find a way to kindly remind your

supervisor that you have not had a chance to learn that yet, and ask
for someone to please explain it more clearly.

Questions to Ask Yourself
What is important to you in a boss? • Someone who is candid with feedback? • Someone who lets you figure things out on your own?
Notes:
Who can help you think about and practice difficult conversations with your boss before you have them? • Parent? • Career counselor?
Notes:

Questions to Ask Yourself

What can you do to manage your stress in a positive way?
  • Exercise?
  • Count to ten before you react?

Notes:

Exercise 3
Finding success on the Job

Part 1: List the three reasons you joined your organization.
1.
2.
3.

Part 2:
Then ask yourself if all three reasons are still in line with your expectations and why or why not.

1.

2.

3.

Part 3:
Now ask yourself (and/or enlist someone you trust) to brainstorm ways to get things back on track.

1.

2.

3.

Practical Suggestions for Gen Z Supervisors

Be willing to learn from your younger tech-savvy workers and give them opportunities to lead the team in applying their second-nature technology skills to things you have done the same way for a long time. Not only will you give them a sense of contribution and job satisfaction, you may be able to improve processes in the department in ways you might have never imagined before.

- **Be patient.** Remind yourself that your Gen Z worker may need guidance or training. Perhaps your employee just lacks your familiarity with the job, rather than the intelligence or ability to learn.

- **Empathize.** Try to remember when you were just getting started. What kind of instruction did you respond to the best—step-by-step details with some room for mistakes, or impatience, terse criticism, and being taken off the project?

- **Give stretch assignments.** Look for ways to give your Gen Z employees a chance to prove and challenge themselves. Investing in the development of Gen Z workers on the job just makes sense. This generation wants to be trained well and given the opportunity to advance.

- **All your actions matter.** Employees pay close attention to how you conduct yourself. Your behavior and leadership will shape the future of your company and the workplace. A respectful and supportive supervisor will bring out your Gen Z workers' best efforts, and they can become your best long-term assets.

Questions for Supervisors of Gen Z to Consider

What training has been provided or can be offered to ensure that your employees are set up for success?

Notes:

How do you respond when a mistake is made by your employee?

Notes:

How do you recognize and reward your teams?

Notes:

CHAPTER FIVE

Attitudes about Other Generations at Work

There are a lot of opinions floating around out there. So far, I've focused primarily on how the older cohorts—Gen Y, Gen X, and the Baby Boomers—view Gen Z. But how does Gen Z view the other cohorts in return?

Human resources professionals and leaders are increasingly aware of the different qualities that each generation brings to their workforce and the wide range of variables that must be integrated in order to see company success. Misunderstood differences tend to cause conflict, while awareness of differences is a major step toward productive collaboration. Management and workers alike can make conscious efforts to understand the perspectives and strengths of their coworkers. When understanding is achieved, biases can be set aside in the interests of working together for the success of the project, the team, and the company.

Of course, each generation will have difficulty seeing the negative characteristics, or stereotypes, associated with their own generation.

And one could easily imagine that it's harder for one generation to view another with more positive regard than negative. Even so, my research found a number of surprisingly generous intergenerational assessments.

They Said . . . We Said . . .

I invited the study participants to share their opinions about their coworkers in each generational group and asked: ***Considering the multigenerational workplace, what is the BEST thing about each generational group?***

It turns out, some respondents couldn't let go of certain negative biases. The responses, instead of strictly identifying positive things, were a mix of positive, negative, and neutral observations.

How Baby Boomers, Gen X, and Gen Y See Gen Z

In offering their opinions about Gen Z, the Baby Boomers, Gen X, and the Gen Ys noted that Gen Z is indeed young, just starting out, an unknown factor, inexperienced, lacking in knowledge, and the generation of the future.

On the positive side, though, the older three cohorts were quite charitable and expected good things for the future, calling out Gen Z's potential and youthful energy. Many of the respondents shared that Gen Z is:

- *"Competent"*
- *"Confident with technology"*
- *"Open-minded"*
- *"Enthusiastic"*
- *"Hardworking"*
- *"Teachable"*
- *"Innovative"*
- *"Smart"*
- *"Capable"*
- *"More laid-back"*

• *"Respectful"*
• *"Genuine in relationships"*

Less complimentary observations seemed to focus on immaturity, self-centeredness, poor work ethic, and poor interpersonal skills.

Insights About How Each Generation Thinks About Each Other				
	About Gen Z	**About Gen Y**	**About Gen X**	**About Baby Boomers**
Gen Z Female	They are innovative and don't mind challenging the status quo.	They have seen and survived a lot of worldwide change.	They are steady, reliable workers & people.	They began and continue a great deal of the social justice campaigns we know today.
Gen Y Female	Always a step ahead of the technology industry and always looking for ways to incorporate the technology in to projects and tasks	Can always learn from them.	They can show you how to be humble and admit when you are wrong or correct someone properly when they are wrong.	Not afraid to do things outside the box and take risks.
Gen X Male	Are still young and impressionable to teach them good work ethics.	The best work ethics, friendly, down to earth.	Very reasponsible yet loose and easy-going.	Are fun but can be down to business as well.
Baby Boomer Female	Less stressed and more laid back.	Content to do a good job and not necessarily looking to move up therefore constant.	Experienced and usually good about sharing that experience.	Dependable and ambitious (still trying to move up).

How Gen Z Sees Themselves

Members of Gen Z offered some refreshingly honest opinions about themselves as a group. They acknowledge their youth and inexperience and some perceptions related to laziness. However, many Gen Z respondents expect that their new ideas and tech-savvy abilities will get them where they want to go. They feel that they are eager, hardworking, and creative, as well as motivated to reach their potential and focus on their goals.

Gen Z consider themselves:
- Eager
- Hardworking
- Creative
- Motivated

How Gen Z Sees the Other Generation Groups

I also examined how Gen Z views their more senior coworkers. For the most part, Gen Z showed appreciation toward the Baby Boomers for their wisdom, experience, and work ethic, while poking some fun at their "old-fashioned" ways.

Gen Z think that Baby Boomers are:
- Wise
- Knowledgeable
- Driven
- Traditional

Gen Z thinks that Gen X is hardworking and "all right" and understanding of younger generations. They note that Gen X has the traditional workplace values of the Baby Boomers tempered with a friendlier and more fun approach.

Gen Z think that Gen X are:
- Hardworking
- Relatable

- Old-school
- Kinder than Baby Boomers

In considering Gen Y, many members of Gen Z admit to relating more to this generation than to the others, largely in terms of technological savvy and new ideas. They also see that while Gen Y, like themselves, are also just starting to find their own way, they have been able to bridge the gap between their own newness and the older traditions.

Gen Z think that Gen Y are:
- Tech savvy
- Creative
- Similar to themselves
- Mentors and role models

Overall, Gen Z speaks respectfully of their more senior colleagues, and admires the motivation, understanding, and mentoring they provide. As mentioned in the Work Preferences chapter, Gen Z members want to be able to look up to their elders and find high-quality guidance, and they seem to find what they are looking for most of the time. This is good news for those who see the differences and want to use them for collaboration and strength.

Implications for Working Relationships and Career Paths

Workplaces that are staffed by all the generations can find a variety of perspectives that will enable them to imagine and prepare for the future while staying grounded and realistic.

Consider the following statements:

Why do I have to speak with everyone to get business done? Email is so much more efficient and I can put everything in writing and communicate with so many more people all at once. – Gen Z Male

When did speaking to people go out of vogue? Last year, I had to spend a lot of time breaking down walls on my team – over an

email misunderstanding. In the end, we all agreed that you can't really solve conflict through email. So many things can get lost in translation. #pickupthephone – Gen X Female

These new kids are so loud and flippant and always pulling out those phones to tap away, tick tick, wasting time and chatting and trying to one-up each other. – Baby Boomer Male

My older coworkers looking at retirement are really resentful of having to learn new systems, and my new hires are looking around with glazed eyes like we're in the UNIVAC age. Department meetings are such an ordeal. It seems like nobody wants to meet in the middle to get anything done. Our ideas are always downplayed. I guess the younger ones at least try to understand, but our frames of reference are still so different than theirs, I can't span the gaps effectively.
– Gen X Female

An age-diverse workforce may be more likely to see "old-fashioned" as "classic" or "wise." New ideas have fresh perspectives that can be welcomed rather than being dismissed without thoughtful consideration. Intentional exploration of the perspectives of other generations can bring rich understanding of goals and methods, and help everyone figure out constructive ways to arrive at common workplace objectives.

Practical Suggestions for Gen Z Employees

You will soon be the largest generation in the workforce, and as such, you will have a lot of impact on society and the workplace. That is some immense potential and responsibility!

- **Change takes time.** Remember that your more experienced coworkers or managers are viewing the world and the workplace through their own personal experiences, whether good or bad. Their views regarding office culture are based on more traditional, formal, and/or hierarchical structures.
- **Stay focused.** Be willing to learn from positive and negative examples and refuse to let unfavorable circumstances interfere with your good attitude and excellent job performance.

- **Even though tech is everywhere, not everyone loves it or knows it.** Try to keep in mind that your older colleagues aren't as accustomed to the level of technology you're used to. Find ways to share your tech knowledge with them in bite-sized portions.
- **Keep an open mind.** Remember also that they probably have some good tricks up their sleeves that have nothing to do with what you know, so learn all you can about doing things the "analog" way. This also includes personal work habits and interpersonal skills, not just task-related smarts. You just never know what jewels of wisdom you might come across, and there may be a few that you can share that may help everyone.

Questions to Ask Yourself
Do you know what is important to your manager? • Face-time? • Initiative? •What does being on time mean – on time or early?
Notes:

Questions to Ask Yourself

What skills can you learn from your more experienced coworkers?
- Navigating the organizational and/or political culture?
- How to get things done?
- Technical skills

Notes:

What skills can you share with your coworkers?
- Technology know-how?
- Special training?
- A fresh approach or different perspective?

Notes:

Exercise 4
Building a Support Network

Think of two people within your organization who you admire and could help you to learn and grow (one of those people could be your boss).

Arrange to have a conversation with them during a time that does not interfere with your (or their) work responsibilities to share what you admire and ask them if they would be open to helping you to learn more.

Remember to follow up and to thank them for their help. If they decline your request, still be polite and find someone else to ask.

Who will you ask, what will you ask, and when will you ask?
1.
2.

3.

Practical Suggestions for Gen Z Supervisors

Be particularly open to contributions from Gen Z workers that stem from their expertise with technology and their fresh outlook on life.

- **Don't expect they will figure everything out.** Share constructive feedback. Lead Gen Z in developing good life-long work habits by setting clear expectations and offering incentives and examples. Specific feedback and judicious correction are helpful, after you take the time to listen and understand where your younger workers are coming from.

- **Remember to be respectful and kind.** Not everyone responds well to tough love. Ruling by inflexible command-and-control methods is counterproductive when dealing with employees who want to contribute meaningfully and be recognized for the value they add.

- **At the end of the day—their success is your success.** Continue to offer every opportunity to train and cross-train, giving them chances to prove themselves and become an integral part of the team.

Questions for Supervisors of Gen Z to Consider

How often do you provide constructive feedback?

Notes:

Do you have regular meetings with your employees?

Notes:

Do you create an environment where you your employees can voice their own opinions?

Notes:

Questions for Supervisors of Gen Z to Consider
How do you recognize and reward your employees?
Notes:

CHAPTER SIX

Career Advice/Reflection

The most helpful advice I have gotten so far is that I shouldn't dedicate my life to my career just yet because I'm still young, and to remember to have fun in this part of my life because I'm only going to be young once. So perhaps I should consider studying abroad while I'm in college instead of focusing on graduating as soon as I possibly can.

Gen Z Male

It may seem odd to ask 18- to 20-year-olds what career advice they have found most valuable, given that workers in this age group are only a couple of years into their career, if that. However, even young people have dreams and ideas about what they want their futures to look like, and even with brief career tenures they can evaluate whether advice seems likely to get them closer to where they want to go. It was refreshing to learn that even at the beginning their careers, members of Gen Z can still recognize sound wisdom when it is offered by leaders they respect and wish to emulate.

With that in mind, I asked the members of Gen Z about the best advice they've received so far.

Learning from Others: Best Advice Gen Z Has Received

The responses are roughly divided into these categories: career progression, work-life balance, financial management, and getting along. The majority of the advice received centered on how to achieve career success.

The advice that was noted most often included comments such as:

- *"Do what you love"* (18% of responses)
- *"Follow your dreams"* (18% of responses)
- *"Don't give up!"* (15% of responses)
- *"Work hard!"* (8% of responses)
- *"Persevere"* (3% of responses)

Love what you do. Five percent of the *"Do what you love"* comments were accompanied by something along the lines of *"and you won't have to work a day in your life,"* and *"because if you hate your job, it will not matter how much money you make."*

Persevere. Gen Z participants found their best encouragement in sentiments like: "Don't let people tell you that you cannot do it. Do it to prove them wrong." Sticking with school and always improving oneself were also common themes.

Pragmatism. One young woman stated that the best advice she'd ever received was: "Be practical. Don't follow your dreams, follow your plans." Some "getting along" wisdom was also mentioned as part of the most-valued advice.

Money matters. Financial management advice included comments such as: "Be smart with your money," "More income leads to better outcomes," "Never get in debt, save money while you can," and a couple variations of "Get paid for what you do." In terms of work-life balance, several Gen Z respondents indicated that they highly valued words of wisdom about balancing money and passion, including advice such as "Always keep your happiness in mind" and "Choose a good balance between financial security and enjoyment when choosing a college major or career."

Lessons Gen Z Has Learned, so Far…

To get a slightly different perspective on which types of advice members of Gen Z value, I asked them to come up with advice for their younger selves. I asked: *If you could go back in time, what advice would you give yourself at the beginning of your career?*

Always listen to your elders. They have been through what you have gone through.

Never gossip about coworkers or your boss.

Be the person that everyone relies on.

Be creative, friendly and open-minded.

Gen Z Male   Gen Z Female   Gen Z Female   Gen Z Female

Work hard. Interestingly, 13% of the Gen Z respondents said they would tell themselves to "work hard," "do NOT slack off," and "don't be lazy." Eight respondents advised their younger selves that if they worked hard and didn't give up, it would all be worth it.

Have confidence. Six percent of the Gen Z participants, admitted to fears and concerns that they would have to overcome in order to get further down the road. They said they would caution themselves to be more confident, not be scared of people, be more assertive and independent, to just make a choice and do it.

Speak up. Two percent of Gen Z would have told themselves: *"If you don't understand something, just ask!"*

I would remind myself that hard work is going to get me into the best career possible.

Gen Z Female

You're in charge of your career, and where you go.

Gen Z Female

Be strong, work hard, and get your money.

Gen Z Female

Have a plan. Self-reporting revealed mixed messages regarding major decisions that would affect the rest of their lives. Four percent of Gen Z said they would have told themselves it was OK to question their paths and plans, review all their options, and not take the first couple of jobs too seriously. Others, however, advised themselves to find their ultimate goal, choose something they like that they could do for a long time, and stick with it. Four would have started earlier to get ahead of the game.

Take charge of their careers. Expressing the same idea in several different ways, many acknowledged their own responsibility for their own success.

Education matters. Six percent would have told themselves to stay in school, work harder, and finish degrees before pursuing careers. Only one Gen Z male said, "Start seeking promotion and increased responsibility early on and focus less on school (within reason)."

Manage finances wisely. Six percent of Gen Z respondents focused on money with strong reminders to get more of it, save it, and be smart with how they are managing their money. Two percent of the respondents told themselves to invest money in health and happiness.

Learn how to get along with people on the job. For on-the-job and interpersonal skills, there was a nice collection of predictable yet tried-and-true advice. Two percent told themselves to be more willing to take advice and learn new things and a broad range of skills. One percent mentioned the need for better time management.

Other comments about advice that they would give their younger selves included:

- *"Pay attention to small details"*
- *"Stay focused"*
- *"Listen to your advisors"*
- *"Follow the rules"*
- *"Keep your head above the water"*
- *"Stay calm under times of pressure"*
- *"Do not be so sensitive because not everyone is going to care about your feelings or about you"*
- *"Don't get involved with coworkers"*
- *"Focus on your work and don't get too much into their personal lives"*
- *"Trust your gut"*
- *"Stop complaining so much"*
- *"Always challenge yourself"*
- *"Be yourself and respect other people's opinions"*
- *"Be nice to everyone"*
- *"Don't make so many mistakes"*
- *"Be prepared"*

- *"Don't stress"*
- *"Do better"*

Implications for Working Relationships and Career Paths

Gen Z's eyes are wide open in terms of understanding how hard some of their more experienced coworkers have struggled with college debt and bear markets, yet they are still eager to be able to chase their dreams and find success in something they are passionate about. They know their success is up to their own hard work, and at the same time, they recognize that they need to be smart about money and work-life balance.

Practical Suggestions for Gen Z Employees

Remember that you're not required to know everything about everything now—it's just not possible. Don't be shy about asking for guidance and advice, even if you decide that what you were told isn't right for you.

- **Acknowledge your values.** Are you driven to succeed financially or is work-life balance more important to you? Know yourself and honor your priorities, but remember that it is your own hard work and your own choices that will take you where you are going. These two are what you control.
- **Reflect on your future.** Think ahead and try to envision the type of success you would like to see in the future, at work and at home.
- **Be open to opportunity.** You never know when a more experienced perspective might change your whole view of things.

Questions to Ask Yourself

Who can help you with your career planning and provide emotional support and guidance for your career planning?
- Counselor?
- Your supervisor?
- Human resources?
- A family member or a friend?

Notes:

What are the trade-offs you need to make to accomplish your goals?
- Making studying a priority over leisure time?
- Seeking internships?
- Stepping outside your comfort zone?
- Working evenings or weekends?

Notes:

Questions to Ask Yourself
Are you prepared to make the required trade-offs? • Do you have a support system of people to help keep you on track? • Do you have your finances in order?
Notes:

Exercise 5
Creating a Career Planning Map

Sometimes it is helpful to chart you career path. Complete the chart below and then ask for advice about your planning from someone you trust.

1. Understand what you have to offer based on your current role and previous experience

List the skills needed for your current role (perhaps from your job description)
Example: Retail Associate, skills needed: working with customers, communication skills, time management, cashier experience, team player, flexibility

Current Role Title:

_____

_____

_____

_____

_____

_____

_____

Other Title(s) Roles:

_____

_____

_____

_____

_____

_____

2. Understand the requirements for the next role that you are interested in pursuing

List the skills needed for your next role (examples can be found by searching employment websites)
Example: Graphic Designer, skills needed: attention to detail, ability to follow established brand guidelines, strong written and verbal communication skills, adept at design software packages, positive attitude, and a proven team player

Next Role:

_____

_____

_____

_____

_____

_____

_____

_____

3. Identify the training and/or education needed for your next role

Examples can be found by searching job descriptions.
Example: Graphic Designer, training/education needed: Bachelor's degree in Graphic Design. Two years' experience.

_____

_____

_____

_____

_____

_____

_____

_____

4. Identify the gaps in your background and training with the role you are seeking

Review the job description against your own experience and training to identify abilities you have, that are transferrable skills, or that you need to acquire. Note: it does not have match 100%. List the areas where you need to gain more experience.

_____

_____

_____

_____

_____

_____

_____

_____

5. Create a plan to fill the gap

Think about ways that you can learn more about what the job entails and how you can get the experience and training you need.
Example: Information interview with a Graphic Designer, join a graphic design professional organization (seek student membership rates), volunteer to design materials for a social organization, explore internships at design agencies, or speak with someone to help you brainstorm ideas about how to build out your next steps.

_____

_____

_____

_____

_____

_____

_____

Practical Suggestions for Gen Z Supervisors

Above all, remember that your Gen Z workers are just starting out. You can serve as a powerful role model, mentor, coach, and sponsor.

- **Be available to your Gen Z employees.** Let your employees know that you are interested in them and encourage them to ask questions. Make sure you have time set aside to be available to your team and inform them of your availability.

- **Build confidence.** Continue to encourage them to do their very best and acknowledge their contributions. Be available for teaching moments, acting as a sounding board while they try to evaluate and make decisions. Find ways to draw out those who seem to be too insecure and encourage them to step out confidently when they should.

Practical Actions for Supervisors of Gen Z to Consider
Are you modeling the behavior you want to see in your teams?
Notes:
Do you mentor other younger employees (inside or outside your organization)?
Notes:

Practical Actions for Supervisors of Gen Z to Consider
What advice would you give your younger self?
Notes:

CHAPTER SEVEN

Everyone Has Something to Offer

Not all of us got participation trophies. People think that we're all lazy or got things handed to us. I think that takes away from the actual progress that our generation is making socially or the contribution that we will make pretty soon economically.

Gen Z Male

Early in my journey as a scholar, my mentor, Dr. Peter Whitehouse, shared the concept of "intergenerativity" (i.e., sharing change across boundaries that normally separate discourse, and tapping the energy that can result from connecting otherwise divergent fields of human endeavor).[21] As I think about the multigenerational workplace, it's important to understand what can promote "intergenerativity" at work. The key is for both Gen Z workers and their supervisors and coworkers to remember that there is more than one perspective at play, and having a productive and positive growth experience shouldn't be considered an insurmountable obstacle.

Open-mindedness and clear communication about desires and expectations can help pave the way for forward progress. The intention to understand and work together is critical; refusal to engage will reverse any progress. This is true whether you are considering personal development or the success of the team or organization.

Members of Gen Z are eager to get to work and feel optimistic about their opportunities. Many are also willing to commit to an employer for a few years, making it well worth the effort of investing in training and development. While young and inexperienced in some ways, they still have a few areas of expertise to bring to the workplace. Their comfort with and knowledge of technology can bring important advantages to any organization.

Key Takeaways

Happiness, relationships, compensation, and job satisfaction are most important for Gen Z, meaning that a solid work-life balance will be the overriding goal in career decisions. In the same vein, Gen Z believes that the American Dream is highly accessible to them, but they realize that paying for education may be challenging.

As with workers of any age, Gen Z employees want a supervisor who will respect and support them with kindness, good leadership, flexibility, and encouragement. They value mentorship provided by their more experienced and senior coworkers and managers.

A few suggested daily reminders for Gen Z employees in the workplace:

- **People carry biases, but those biases will not prevent you from succeeding if you're persistent and determined enough.** Remember that your boss might be viewing you with expectations he or she would place upon his more experienced employees, or with other implicit biases. This may not be fair, but many studies show that it exists.
- **You are in control of your destiny.** You have an opportunity to prove yourself or to make a choice to find another role.
- **Everyone can grow.** Continue to do your best. Be sure to ask for the information and training you need to understand how to be successful in your role, and find ways to contribute to the success of the company.
- **Careers are journeys and setbacks can provide valuable growth and lessons for you.** In many cases, your first few jobs may not be

career material. There's something to be learned at every job, so do your best at each stop, and you'll be highly qualified to step into your ideal position when it comes along.

- **Have a plan.** If you have intentions to stay with your employer, it will be important to have a plan for short-term and long-term success. In most cases, it will be up to you to make that plan. Seek help from experienced coworkers, your human resources department, or a mentor.
- **It is OK if you have not figured everything out yet.** At this point in your life, time is on your side. Having a plan can be helpful and asking for help and advice is a smart move to make. It's OK to be in transition and to keep figuring things out.
- **Your success is in your own capable hands!** You have a lot to offer. Work hard and don't be discouraged by those who tell you that you cannot achieve your goals.

Suggested Actions for Gen Z to Take

Create a mindset for success. Setbacks and victories are a part of every career. Every time you think of a reason why something cannot happen, balance it with a reason why it can happen. Create a blueprint for your career that will allow to you be open to opportunity and prepared to take on new challenges.

Build a support system. It can include friends, family, coworkers, and mentors, social or professional organizations.

Save for the future. Saving money and living within your means are great habits and can allow you greater flexibility to make decisions about your life and career.

A few suggested daily reminders for Supervisors of Gen Z in the workplace:

Remember that your Gen Z employee is young, inexperienced in life and work, and simply does not know everything your more seasoned workers do at this point in their careers. Try to view their less than ideal behavior as what it most likely is: youth, passion, or uncertainty, and not lazy or willful interference with your goals.

- **Assume good intentions.** Everyone has something to offer and to learn.

- **Be a great role model.** It's your job to model good communication and work habits, and Gen Z workers want a boss they can respect and emulate.

Actions for Supervisors of Gen Z to Consider

- **Provide frameworks for how to achieve the goals and objectives you are seeking.** My research suggests that Gen Z will benefit from a framework that gives them a good idea of how the role or opportunity aligns to their needs for compensation and growth. So give them the development environment they need to accomplish their goals.

- **Provide training.** Engage your young workers with suitable training and extra challenges. Let them add value to the team with their unique skills.

- **Be open to sharing ongoing constructive feedback.** Be sure to acknowledge successful contributions and give positive feedback and guidance in the face of failure.

- **Remember that Gen Z is highly motivated to do well.** However, they are pragmatic, perhaps in part due to their experience in the world, the availability of technology, and instantly accessible information. Encourage each employee to reach for more.

Finally

Gen Z is well educated, sensible, and ready to have a major impact on the labor force in the next few years. On the whole, most members of Gen Z remain optimistic. They have witnessed the impact of the economic bust on Baby Boomers, Gen X, and Millennials family members, so they are realistic, practical, and rightly cautious.

Nonetheless, their sense of hope is strong, and they believe that great accomplishments are possible. Equipped with the latest technology, the ability to quickly access information about virtually anything they want to know, and a keen understanding of the diverse perspectives of their peers, this generation is set to influence what makes society thrive.

My research results were eye-opening and heartening in the sense that they presented a mostly positive outlook for the up-and-coming generation in the American workforce.

To boil it down, the best results can be achieved when both workers and supervisors commit to clear communication while resisting the urge to merely defend one's own position. When all sides' views are understood, everyone is better able to pursue solutions that honor every perspective and still get the job done.

Generation Z promises to breathe new life into the evolving workforce. They are realistic, practical, optimistic, and hopeful. Members of Gen Z are well prepared for the challenges that lie ahead, and they will soon begin making great contributions to the American workplace.

Action Plan for Gen Z: Summary of Exercises

Exercise 1
Preparing for Success

What questions will you ask your supervisor about how to be successful in your current role?
Notes:

Exercise 2
Setting Priorities

List the top three things that will be important for you (personally and/or professionally) in the next six to 12 months and then have at least two conversations with someone you trust about how you accomplish these goals.
1.

2.
3.

Exercise 3
Finding Success on Your Job

Part 1: List the three reasons you joined your organization.
1.
2.

3.

Part 2: Then ask yourself if all three reasons are still in line with your expectations and why or why not.

1.

2.

Part 3: Now ask yourself (and/or enlist someone you trust) to brainstorm ways to get things back on track.

1.

2.

3.

Exercise 4
Building a Support Network

Think of two people within your organization that you admire and could help you to learn and grow (one of those people could be your boss; if it is your boss's manager, you may want to get the support of your boss first).

Arrange to have a conversation with them during a time that does not interfere with your (or their) work responsibilities to share what you admire and ask them if they would be open to helping you to learn more.

Remember to follow up and to thank them for their help. If they reject your request, be polite and find someone else to ask.

Who will you ask, what will you ask, and when will you ask?
1.
2.
3.

Exercise 5
Creating a Career Planning Map

Sometimes it is helpful to chart your career path. Complete the chart below and then ask for advice about your planning from someone you trust.

1. Understand what you have to offer based on your current role and previous experience

List the skills needed for your current role (perhaps from your job description)
Example: Retail Associate, skills needed: working with customers, communication skills, time management, cashier experience, team player, flexibility

Current Role Title:

_____

_____

_____

_____

_____

_____

Other Title(s) Roles:

_____

_____

_____

_____

_____

_____

2. Understand the requirements for the next role that you are interested in pursuing

> **List the skills needed for your next role (examples can be found by searching employment websites)**
> *Example: Graphic Designer, skills needed: attention to detail, ability to follow established brand guidelines, strong written and verbal communication skills, adept at design software packages, positive attitude, and a proven team player*
>
> *Next Role:* _____
>
> _____
>
> _____
>
> _____
>
> _____
>
> _____

3. Identify the training and/or education needed for your next role

> **Examples can be found by searching job descriptions.**
> *Example: Graphic Designer, training/education needed: Bachelor's degree in Graphic Design. Two years' experience.*
>
> _____
>
> _____
>
> _____
>
> _____
>
> _____
>
> _____

4. Identify the gaps in your background and training with the role you are seeking

> **Review the job description against your own experience and training to identify abilities you have, that are transferrable skills, or that you need to acquire. Note: it does not have to match 100%.**

List the areas where you need to gain more experience.

_____

_____

_____

_____

_____

_____

5. Create a plan to fill the gap

Think about ways that you can learn more about what the job entails and how you can get the experience and training you need.
Example: Information interview with a Graphic Designer, join a graphic design professional organization (seek student membership rates), volunteer to design materials for a social organization, explore internships at design agencies, or speak with someone to help you brainstorm ideas about how to build out your next steps.

_____

_____

_____

_____

_____

_____

Checklist for Supervisors of Gen Z

- **Teach the basics and be a coach.** Think of ways to encourage the practical aspects of career advancement, like good work habits and skills that will serve them well in any job.
- **Show them the money.** Frequently remind them about the connection between their performance and the rewards they can expect, such as promotions, recognition, bonuses, and premium shifts.
- **Let them know that they are valued.** Give your Gen Z workers the opportunity to grow and advance, while making sure they know they are important to the success of the company.
- **Be clear about the next steps.** Your management style and support of their development and their ability to achieve their goals will play a huge role in their decision to stay or go.
- **If promotions are not available, make sure growth is an option.** Manage expectations by being transparent regarding the path toward greater opportunities and growth.
- **Gen Z is pragmatic and not shy about moving on.** Be prepared for them to move on when their goals outstrip what you can offer them.
- **Be patient.** Remind yourself that your Gen Z worker may need guidance or training.
- **Empathize.** Try to remember when you were just getting started.
- **Give stretch assignments.** This generation wants to be trained well and given the opportunity to advance.
- **All your actions matter.** Your behavior will shape and set the tone for the workplace.
- **Don't expect they will figure everything out.** Share constructive feedback. Specific feedback and judicious correction are helpful.
- **Remember to be respectful and kind.** Inflexible command-and-control methods are counterproductive with employees who want

to contribute meaningfully and be recognized for the value they add.

- **At the end of the day—their success is your success.** Continue to train and cross-train, giving them chances to prove themselves and become an integral part of the team.

- **Be available to your Gen Z employees.** Make sure you have time set aside to be available to your team and inform them of your availability.

- **Build confidence.** Continue to encourage them to do their very best and acknowledge their contributions. Find ways to draw out those who seem to be too insecure and encourage them to step out confidently when they should.

About the Generations in the Workplace Series

This book series is based on the findings of a study that was conducted in the fall of 2016, to identify what is important to employees in the multigenerational workplace. The goal of the series is to provide practical advice to professionals as they navigate their careers and to serve as a resource for managers and coworkers within age-diverse workforces.

About 1,000 U.S. citizens born between 1946 and 1998 responded to a survey that was professionally facilitated by an independent research organization. The final validated sample for this study included nearly 700 employed individuals who were college graduates (Baby Boomers, Gen Z, and Gen Y) and employed college students (Gen Z). The gender makeup in the sample was split 50/50 male/female. Twenty-eight percent of the sample were members of Generation Z.

The study included a 35-question multiple choice survey in which the respondents were asked to select the best answer, rank a series of concepts, or write in a response to certain questions. I also conducted interviews with members of Gen Z. The core questions I wanted to explore were:

- What values are foundational to each generation's motivations?
- How do the respondents feel about their career as well as their personal and professional values?
- How do employees of each generation perceive and interact with those of other generations?
- What does each generation want from their supervisor to make them more successful in their role?

Most specifically, I wanted to explore the factors that help people succeed in their careers, and to determine how individuals and organizations achieve goals in multigenerational workplaces.

After reviewing several previous studies on the generational cohorts, I chose these birth years to represent the groups identified in the research for this book:

- Baby Boomer 1946–1964: ages 52–70*
- Gen X 1965–1980: ages 36–51
- Gen Y (Millennials) 1981–1995: ages 21–35
- Gen Z born after 1995: ages 20 and under**

* Age at the time of the study
** The study included only 18- to 20-year-old participants

References

1. Bernard, D. (2012, June 15). 8 Scary retirement facts. US News and World Report. Retrieved from http://money.usnews.com/money/blogs/on-retirement/2012/06/15/8-scary-retirement-facts

2. Horovitz, B. (2012, May 4). After Gen X, Millennials, what should next generation be? USA Today. Retrieved from http://usatoday30.usatoday.com/money/advertising/story/2012-05-03/naming-the-next-generation/54737518/1

3. Top 10 Gen Z and IGen questions answered. (2016). The Center for Generational Kinetics. Retrieved from http://genhq.com/igen-gen-z-generation-z-centennials-info/

4. Finley, P. D. (2016). Diversity is no longer a workforce issue; for Gen Z, it is the workforce. Diversity in Steam Magazine. Retrieved from http://diversityinsteam.com/trending/diversity-is-no-longer-a-workforce-issue-for-gen-z-it-is-the-workforce/

5. Dill, K.N. (2015, November 6). 7 Things employers should know about the Gen Z workforce. Forbes. Retrieved from http://www.forbes.com/sites/kathryndill/2015/11/06/7-things-employers-should-know-about-the-gen-z-workforce

6. Pew Research Center. (2016, October 6). The state of American jobs. Pew Research Center. Retrieved from http://www.pewsocialtrends.org/2016/10/06/the-state-of-american-jobs/

7. Pew Research Center (2016 October 6). Change in the American workplace. Pew Research Center. Retrieved from http://www.pewsocialtrends.org/2016/10/06/1-changes-in-the-american-workplace/

8. Looper, L. (2011, May 23). How Generation Z works. HowStuffWorks.com. Retrieved from http://people.howstuffworks.com/culture-traditions/generation-gaps/generation-z.htm

9. Singh, S. (2014, May 12). The 10 social and tech trends that could shape the next decade. Forbes. Retrieved from http://www.forbes.com/sites/sarwantsingh/2014/05/12/the-top-10-mega-trends-of-the-decade/#65a24c9c560a

10. Infographic. (2015, October). Gen Z's stance on politics. The Center for Generational Kinetics. Retrieved from http://genhq.com/igen-gen-z-stance-on-politics-infographic

11. Leonard, B. (2015, January 12). Survey compares workplace traits of generations Y and Z. Society for Human Resource Management. Retrieved from https://www.shrm.org/hr-today/news/hr-news/pages/generation-z-traits.aspx

12. Adams, J. T. (1931). The Epic of America, Boston, MA: Little, Brown & Company.

13. Press release. (2016, June 24). American Time Use Survey Summary. U.S. Department of Labor. Retrieved from http://www.bls.gov/news.release/atus.nr0.htm

14. Key findings. (2013, July 15). 2013 U.S. Workplace study. Gensler. Retrieved from http://www.gensler.com/research-insight/research/the-2013-us-workplace-survey-1?q=us%20workplace%20survey

15. Schawbel, D. (2014, September 2). Gen Y and Gen Z global workplace expectations study. Millennial Branding. Retrieved from http://millennialbranding.com/2014/geny-genz-global-workplace-expectations-study/

16. Kena, G., Hussar, W., McFarland, J., de Brey C., Musu-Gillette, L., Wang, X. ... Dunlop Velez, E. (2016, May 26). The condition of education. National Center for Education Statistics. Retrieved from http://nces.ed.gov/programs/coe/indicator_cha.asp

17. Study report. (2016). Getting to know Gen Z: exploring middle and high schoolers' expectations for higher education. Barnes & Noble College. Retrieved from http://next.bncollege.com/wp-content/uploads/2015/10/Gen-Z-Research-Report-Final.pdf

18. Press release. (2016, September 22). Employee tenure in 2016. Bureau of Labor Statistics. Retrieved from http://www.bls.gov/news.release/pdf/tenure.pdf

19. Wegman, L. A., Hoffman, B. J., Carter, N. T., Twenge, J.M., Guenole, N. (2016). Placing job characteristics in context: cross-temporal meta-analysis of changes in job characteristics since 1965. Journal of Management, 20(10), 1-35.

20. Amabile, T. M., Conti, R., Coon, H., Lazenby, J., and Herron, M. (1996, October). Assessing the work environment for creativity. Academy of Management Journal 39, no. 5. Retrieved from http://people.wku.edu/ richard.miller/amabile.pdf

21. George, D., Whitehouse, C., Whitehouse, P. (2011). A model of intergenerativity: how the intergenerational school is bringing the generations together to foster collective wisdom and community health. Journal of Intergenerational Relationships, 9:4, 389-404. Retrieved from https://www.healthandenvironment.org/docs/WhitehouseA_Model_of_ Intergenerativity.pdf

About the Author

Dr. Candace Steele Flippin lives by the philosophy that bringing multiple perspectives to the table results in better outcomes. An award-winning public affairs executive, she has worked at Fortune 500 companies, a global public relations agency, and national non-profit organizations. She is also a Research Fellow at the Weatherhead School of Management at Case Western Reserve University, where she researches the multigenerational workplace.

CPSIA information can be obtained
at www.ICGtesting.com
Printed in the USA
FFOW01n1056240517
35890FF